Sierra Nevada Network Bird Monitoring

2011 Annual Report

Natural Resource Data Series NPS/SIEN/NRDS—2012/362

Amanda L. Holmgren, Robert L. Wilkerson, and Rodney B. Siegel

The Institute for Bird Populations
P.O. Box 1346
Point Reyes Station, CA 94956

September 2012

U.S. Department of the Interior
National Park Service
Natural Resource Stewardship and Science
Fort Collins, Colorado

The National Park Service, Natural Resource Stewardship and Science office in Fort Collins, Colorado, publishes a range of reports that address natural resource topics. These reports are of interest and applicability to a broad audience in the National Park Service and others in natural resource management, including scientists, conservation and environmental constituencies, and the public.

The Natural Resource Data Series is intended for the timely release of basic data sets and data summaries. Care has been taken to assure accuracy of raw data values, but a thorough analysis and interpretation of the data has not been completed. Consequently, the initial analyses of data in this report are provisional and subject to change.

All manuscripts in the series receive the appropriate level of peer review to ensure that the information is scientifically credible, technically accurate, appropriately written for the intended audience, and designed and published in a professional manner.

Data in this report were collected and analyzed using methods based on established, peer-reviewed protocols and were analyzed and interpreted within the guidelines of the protocols. This report received informal peer review by subject-matter experts who were not directly involved in the collection, analysis, or reporting of the data.

Views, statements, findings, conclusions, recommendations, and data in this report do not necessarily reflect views and policies of the National Park Service, U.S. Department of the Interior. Mention of trade names or commercial products does not constitute endorsement or recommendation for use by the U.S. Government.

This report is available from the Sierra Nevada Network website (http://science.nature.nps.gov/im/units/sien/)and the Natural Resource Publications Management website (http://www.nature.nps.gov/publications/nrpm/).

Please cite this publication as:

Holmgren, A. L., R. L. Wilkerson, and R. B. Siegel. 2012. Sierra Nevada Network bird monitoring: 2011 annual report. Natural Resource Data Series NPS/SIEN/NRDS—2012/362. National Park Service, Fort Collins, Colorado.

NPS 963/116865, September 2012

Contents

Figures

Tables

Executive Summary

In 2011, we completed the first field season of long-term bird monitoring associated with the Inventory and Monitoring Program of the Sierra Nevada Network (SIEN). Field work included data collection on the annual panel as well as the first of four alternating panels. Crews conducted 744 point counts at point count survey stations located along 51 transects in Sequoia and Kings Canyon National Parks (SEKI) and Yosemite National Park (YOSE). The average number of points visited per transect was 14.6 (range = 10-22 points per transect). We also completed surveys at the 42 point count stations at Devils Postpile National Monument (DEPO), which are arranged in a grid pattern. We detected 121 bird species in the two large parks, 96 of which were detected during one or more point counts, and the remainder of which were detected by our crew members only at times other than during point counts. For the 72 species that were detected during three or more point counts on annual-panel transects in 2011, we present the total number of detections on annual-panel transects in each park during the 2011 field season. We detected 42 bird species during point counts at DEPO. We present the number of detections, and the number of point counts with detections, for each species detected during point counts at DEPO. These data, along with data collected in future years, will be adjusted for differences in survey effort or detection probability in conjunction with our 4-year trend analyses.

We faced a very challenging first year due to high stream crossings, an unusually deep snowpack, and extremely late-lingering snow, which delayed or even prevented access to many of our middle and high-elevation transects. Nevertheless, preliminary results indicate the SIEN Bird Monitoring Project will yield robust sample sizes for many species when we conduct trend analyses after every fourth year. Observed changes in bird populations that we find in subsequent years, when analyzed in the context of annual weather variation and perhaps other factors, will yield useful findings about the drivers of population dynamics in birds of the SIEN, and are likely to spur additional targeted research and help refine management priorities and needs within the parks.

Acknowledgments

We thank the 2011 crew members for their hard work and dedication to the project: R. Carlton, Z. Kuspa, D. Mauer, S. Price, and D. Wolfson. We thank M. Rose for her contributions toward developing the SIEN bird monitoring protocol. A. Chung-MacCoubrey supported all aspects of the project, providing leadership and assistance from beginning to end. S. Graban was helpful in countless ways, most notably in acquiring and preparing field gear, GPS support, detailed logistical support, and moral support. L. Chow was immensely important in formatting the project database and also helped with gear and logistical support in Yosemite. We thank S. Stock for logistical assistance, advice, and support at Yosemite, and D. Dulen for help and support at Devils Postpile. We thank M. Tingley for computer programming support, and the ESRI Conservation Program for software support. This project was funded by the SIEN Inventory and Monitoring Program and conducted by The Institute for Bird Populations' Sierra Nevada Bird Observatory. This is Contribution No. 438 of The Institute for Bird Populations.

Introduction

Across the United States, many populations of birds are now threatened or endangered, or will likely become threatened soon, as a result of anthropogenic climate change and other environmental stressors (North American Bird Conservation Initiative 2009). Conservation and management of habitats on public lands plays a particularly important role in the conservation of these populations (North American Bird Conservation Initiative, U.S. Committee, 2011).

Sierra Nevada Network parks provide birds over 658,000 hectares (1,600,000 acres) of unusually diverse habitats, ranging from gently sloping foothill grasslands up to windswept alpine wetlands and peaks. National park units in the Sierra Nevada Network collectively range in elevation from around 400 m in the foothills, to 4,418 m at the top of Mt. Whitney, and contain vast tracts of mid-elevation and subalpine conifer forest, as well as substantial acreage of chaparral, oak woodland and savanna, groves of giant sequoia, upland hardwood forest, meadows and streamside vegetation, and alpine plant communities. While none of the approximately 200 bird species that breed, winter, or migrate through the Sierra Nevada are endemic to the range, the key to its exceptional bird diversity is its extreme elevation gradient and corresponding habitat diversity—the Sierra Nevada supports the most diverse assortment of terrestrial habitats and birds of any bioregion in California (Beedy 1985).

SIEN parks fulfill vital roles as refuges for bird species dependent on late successional forest conditions, and as reference sites for assessing the effects of land use and land cover changes on bird populations throughout the Sierra Nevada region (Silsbee and Peterson 1991, Siegel et al. 2011). These regional landscape changes may result from activities such as land conversion and forest management, or from broader-scale processes such as global climate change. Indeed, monitoring population trends at 'control' sites, i.e., national parks, is especially important because the parks are among the few sites in the United States where population trends due to large-scale regional or global change patterns are relatively unconfounded by local changes in land-use (Simons et al. 1999).

SIEN parks also provide critical laboratories for assessing the effects of climate change on Sierra Nevada birds (Siegel et al. 2011). Mountain-dwelling birds have already responded to climate change in many parts of the world by shifting their ranges upslope (Pounds et al. 1999, Root et al. 2003, Root et al. 2005). In the Sierra Nevada, Tingley et al. (2009) found evidence that the distributions of many bird species have changed during the past century, and tied many of those changes to local changes in temperature and precipitation.

SIEN selected bird populations as a vital sign and surrogate for evaluation of network ecosystem condition in Sierra Nevada Network parks for the following reasons:

1. Birds occupy a wide diversity of ecological niches in Sierra parks.

2. Relative to other animal taxa, birds are conspicuous, easily observable, and monitoring is cost effective.

3. Knowledge of the natural history of many bird species has a rich basis in literature.

4. All units in SIEN have a strong foundation of inventory data (Siegel and DeSante 2002, Siegel and Wilkerson 2004, 2005a, Heath 2004, 2005) upon which to build future monitoring efforts.

5. Monitoring Avian Productivity and Survivorship (MAPS) has occurred at all parks for varying numbers of years and time periods, including at one station in Yosemite (Hodgdon Meadows) since 1990 (e.g., DeSante 1995, 2005; DeSante et al. 2004, 2005; Siegel et al. 2007a, 2007d; Gates and Heath 2003; Heath 2004, 2005, 2007).

6. Bird monitoring is particularly efficient, in the sense that dozens of species can be monitored simultaneously with the same survey protocol, and costs are relatively low.

7. Birds generally occupy a high position on the food web–secondary consumers (i.e., insectivores)–making them good indicators of ecosystem change (Furness et al. 1993, Greenwood et al. 1993).

8. Bird monitoring across all park ecosystems can serve as an indicator of change at the community level.

The primary goal of long-term bird monitoring in the SIEN is to assess park-wide and Network-wide bird population trends by monitoring population densities across the parks' diverse habitats and broad habitat gradients. Results from this long-term monitoring of birds throughout the Network should provide information to inform future decisions on important management issues, including fire management, meadow restoration, the effects of introduced species, visitor impacts, and even the bolstering of resistance and resilience to climate change (Steel et al. 2012).

This annual report on bird monitoring in the SIEN contains minimal data analysis and is intended primarily as a basic data summary. More comprehensive analyses of the data, including trend analysis that accounts for the potentially confounding effects of variation in detectability and sampling effort, will be conducted in conjunction with trend analyses conducted after every fourth year of sampling. Until then, the results presented in this report should be considered provisional.

Study Area

The study area for the long-term bird monitoring in the SIEN (Figure 1) includes areas of SEKI and YOSE that are accessible by foot and lie within 1.625 km of a road or trail, as well as all of DEPO.

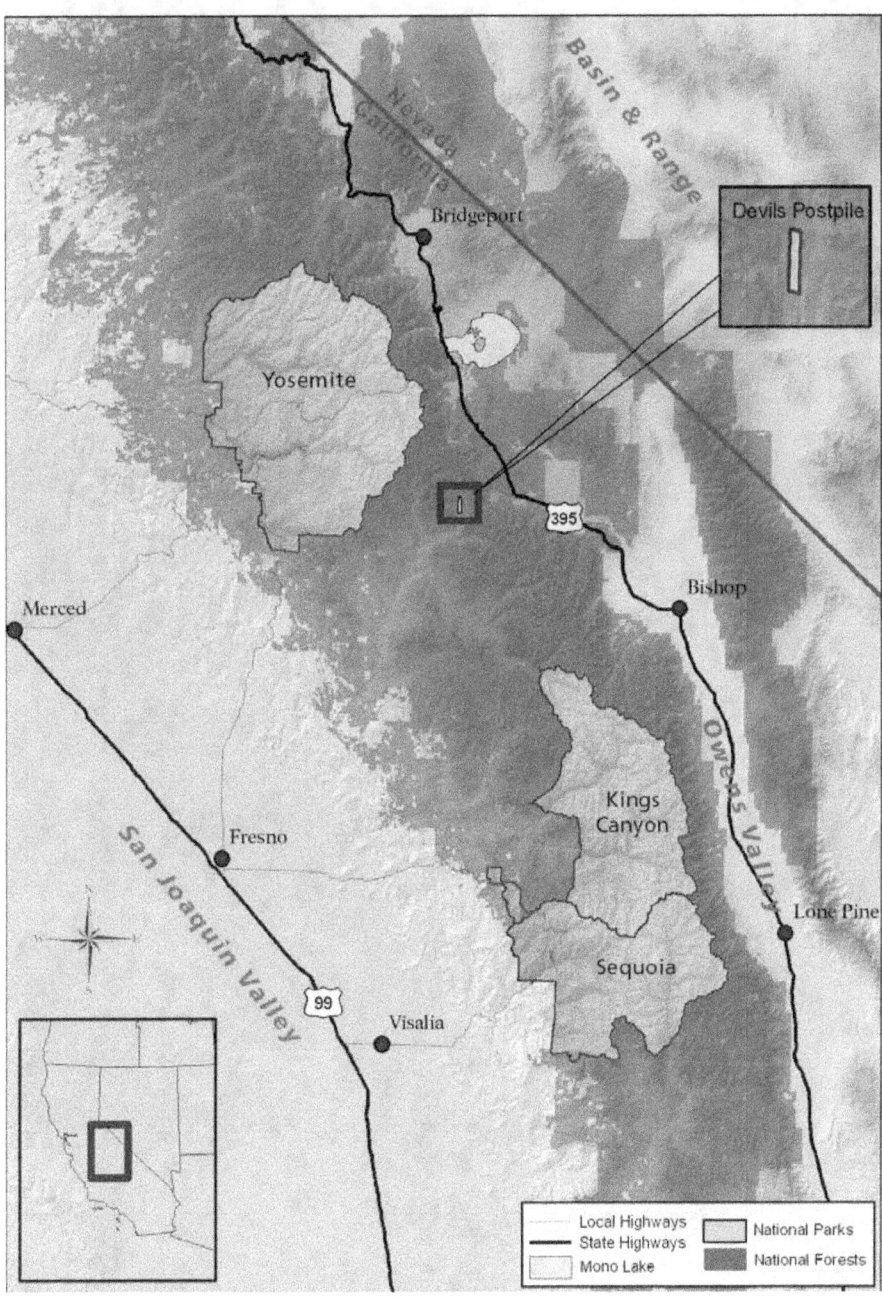

Figure 1. National Park Service units in the SIEN, all of which are participating in the Network's long-term bird monitoring project.

Methods

Siegel et al. (2010) provide a detailed description of the sample design for long-term bird monitoring in the SIEN. In brief, the sample design for the two large parks utilizes five panels of transects in each park. At SEKI each panel includes one low-elevation transect (transect starting points < 1,600 m), nine mid-elevation transects (transect starting points between 1,600 m and 3,000 m) and five high-elevation transects (transect starting points >3,000 m). At YOSE each panel includes five low-elevation transects (transect starting points <1,800 m), five mid-elevation transects (transect starting points between 1,800 m and 2,750 m), and five high-elevation transects (transect starting points >2,750 m). All transect starting points are on park trails, and the transects consist of a line of approximately 14 points, half of which extend perpendicularly (or as close to perpendicularly as topographic and physiographic features allow) in each direction away from the trail.

In 2011 we implemented the full study design in the two large parks for the first year, including surveys of the annual panel ('Ann1') as well as the first alternating panel ('Alt2'; Figures 2-3). We also surveyed DEPO in 2011, where the sample design consists of a nearly systematic grid of point count survey stations to be surveyed every year (Figure 4).

Crew Training and Certification

David Wolfson, a Seasonal Biologist with The Institute for Bird Populations (IBP), served as the 2011 Field Lead. David began training three field technicians on April 28, with assistance from IBP Staff Biologist and Project Co-lead Bob Wilkerson. Rodney Siegel (IBP Research Scientist and Project Co-lead/Principal Investigator), Dayna Mauer (IBP Seasonal Biologist), and Alice Chung-MacCoubrey (SIEN Inventory & Monitoring Program Manager) also participated in the training session. Training followed guidelines described in the SIEN bird monitoring protocol (Siegel et al. 2010), and required crew members to confidently identify all regularly occurring bird species in the parks by sight and especially sound. By the end of the official training session on May 14, two of the three field technicians had passed the rigorous point count certification exam and were ready to begin collecting data. After additional study and practice, the one remaining field technician was also certified. All individuals who collected data during the 2011 field season (Table 1) were employees, contract biologists, or field biologist interns of The Institute for Bird Populations.

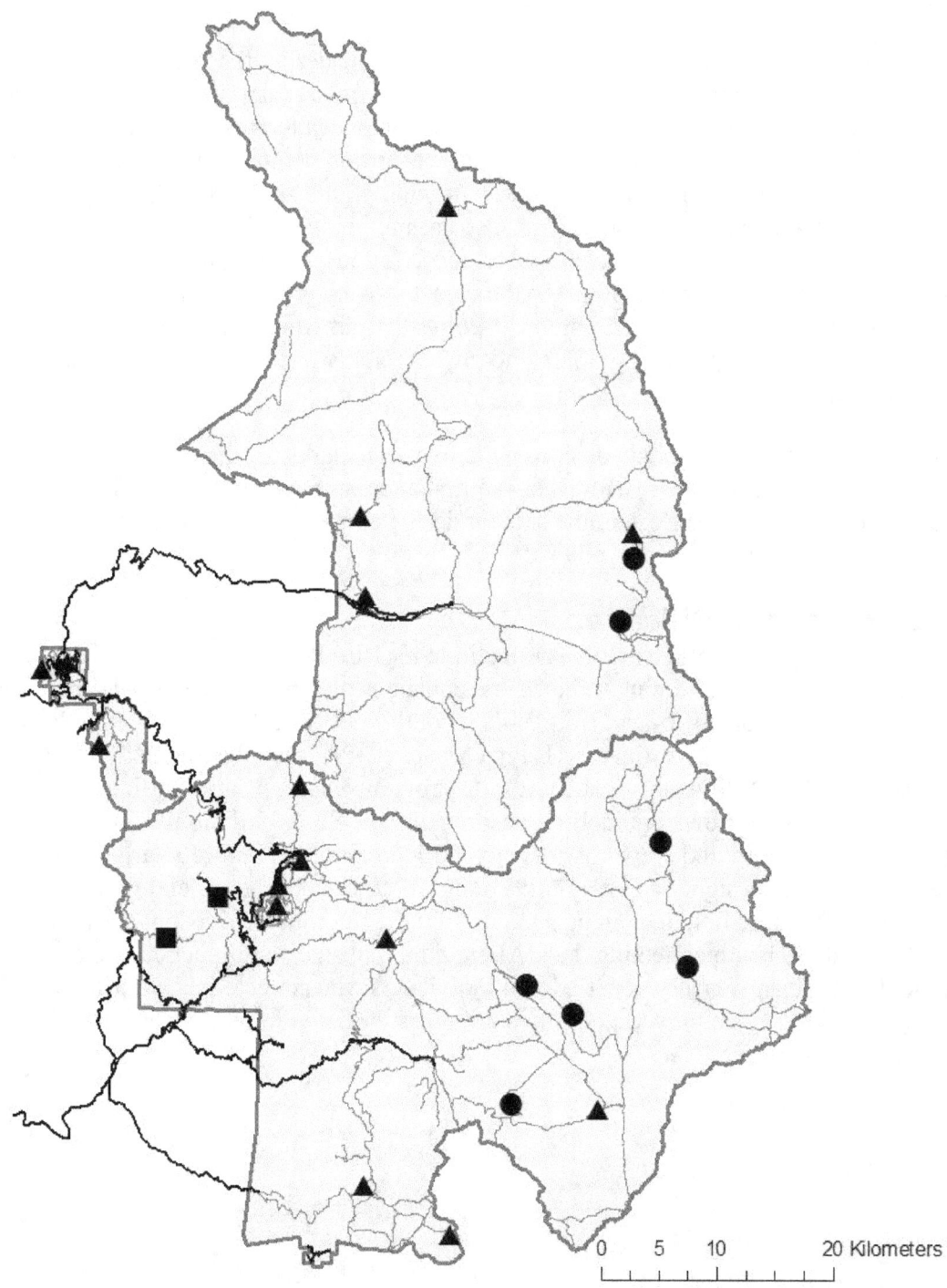

Figure 2. Approximate locations of transects conducted at SEKI in 2011. Squares indicate low-elevation transects, triangles indicate mid-elevation transects, and circles indicate high-elevation transects. Black lines indicate roads and brown lines indicate trails. Gray line indicates the parks' boundaries.

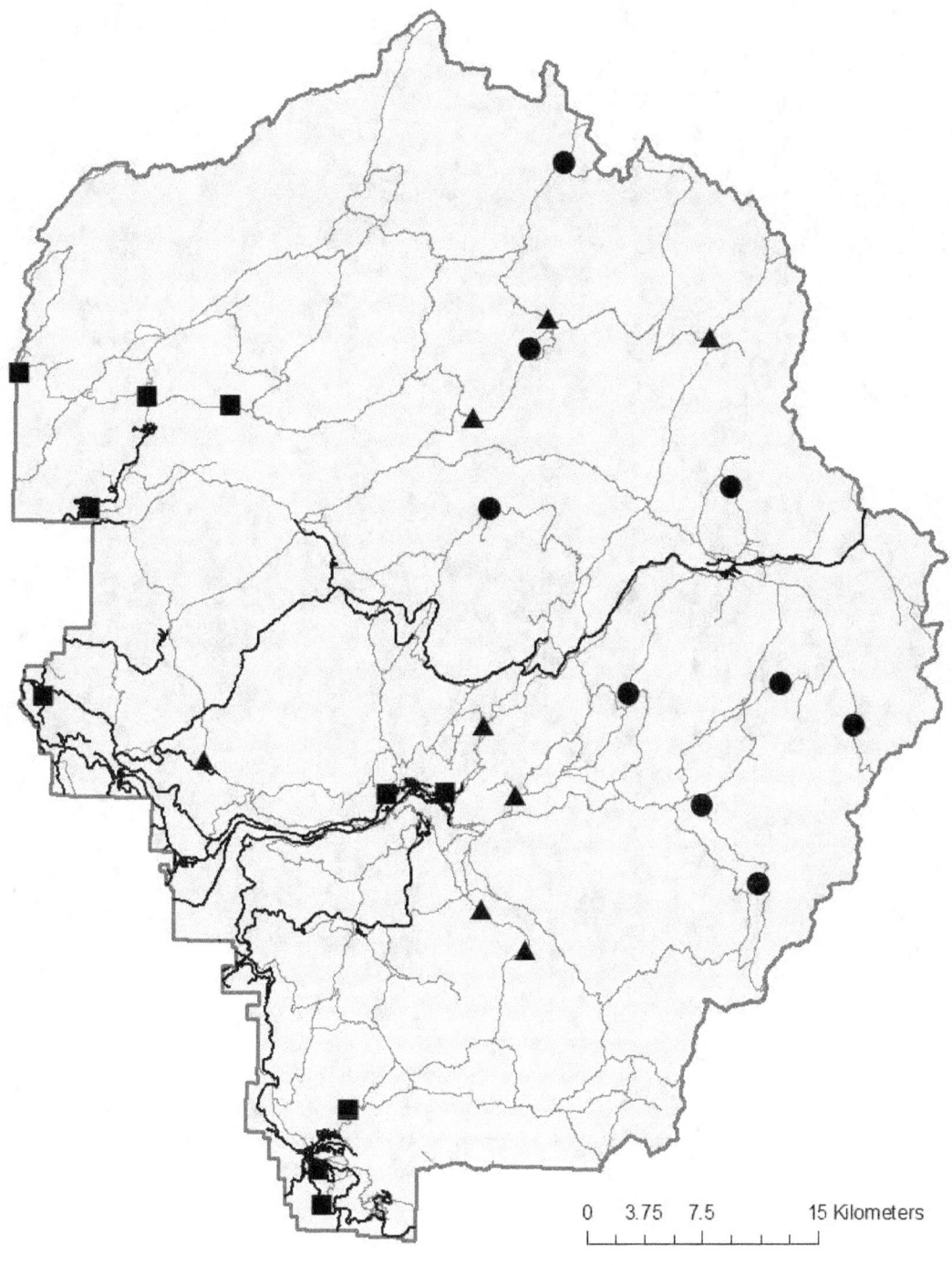

Figure 3. Approximate locations of transects conducted at YOSE in 2011. Squares indicate low-elevation transects, triangles indicate mid-elevation transects, and circles indicate high-elevation transects. Black lines indicate roads and brown lines indicate trails. Gray line indicates the park boundary.

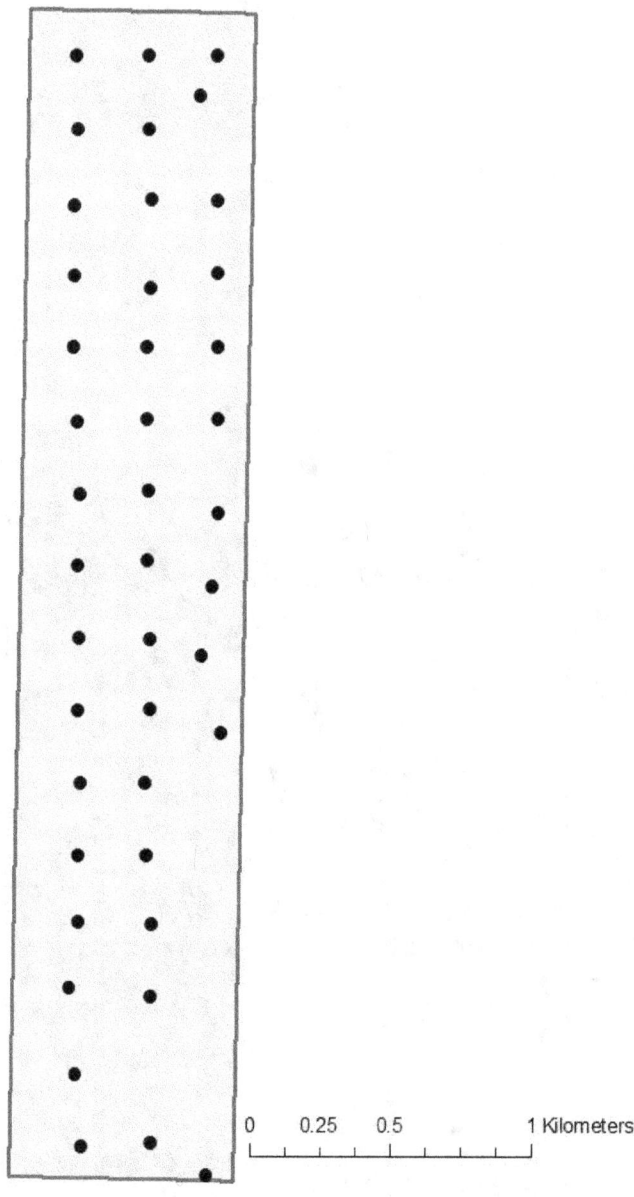

Figure 4. Locations of point count stations surveyed at DEPO in 2011. Gray line indicates the park boundary.

Table 1. Observers who conducted point counts in the SIEN in 2011 (in alphabetical order).

Observer	Role
Samantha Barnett	Technician
Ryan Carlton	Technician
Zeka Kuspa	Technician
Dayna Mauer	Technician
Rodney Siegel	Project co-lead/Principal investigator
Bob Wilkerson	Project co-lead
David Wolfson	Field Lead

Data Collection

All point count data were collected between July 8 and July 10 at DEPO, between May 29 and July 23 at SEKI, and between May 19 and July 23 at YOSE. At the two large parks, low-elevation transects were generally surveyed first, followed by the mid-elevation transects, and finally the high-elevation transects.

Data collection followed the detailed procedures explained in the SIEN bird monitoring protocol (Siegel et al. 2010). Crew members generally worked in pairs to survey a single transect each morning. Crew members were provided with maps and coordinates indicating the location of transect 'starting points', which lay directly on trails. Beginning within 10 minutes of official sunrise, each observer conducted a point count, and then continued along the transect route, conducting another point count every 250 m until 3.5 hours after official local sunrise. Crew members began from the indicated starting points, and then established transect routes according to the guidelines in Siegel et al. (2010).

At each point count station observers recorded the starting time, scored the degree of noise interference caused by such factors as flowing water or wind, recorded the weather conditions, and then began the seven-minute point count. The seven-minute point count was broken into three time intervals (0-3:00, 3:01-5:00, and 5:01-7:00). Observers noted each time interval in which they detected each individual bird. Birds observed in the first three minutes allow comparison with Breeding Bird Survey data (Sauer et al. 2008), which are based on three-minute counts. Observers estimated the horizontal distance, to the nearest meter, to each bird detected. The observers also recorded whether the distance estimates were based on an aural or visual detection, and whether the bird ever sang a territorial song during the point count.

After completing their last point count each morning, observers retraced their steps back to the starting point. Along the way they collected habitat information at each of the survey stations classifying the habitat in a 50-m radius circle according to the California Wildlife Habitats Relationship system (Mayer and William F. Laudenslayer 1988). During subsequent visits to these points, observers will verify that the habitat classification is correct, and/or note any substantial changes. While conducting the habitat assessments, observers also used Global Positioning System (GPS) units to collect location data files and record descriptive information and photos to facilitate locating the survey points during future survey visits.

Whenever crew members detected species thought to be rare in the park or difficult to detect during diurnal point count surveys, they completed "Rare Bird Report Forms", including descriptions of the birds' appearance, behavior, and precise location. These reports covered not only birds detected during point counts, but also birds detected while sampling vegetation, hiking between transects, relaxing at camp in the evening, or at any other time during the field season, including the pre-season training session. Additionally, a comprehensive list of all incidental species observations was updated by the field crew each time a new species was detected within park boundaries.

After completing their fieldwork each day, partners reviewed each other's data forms for missing or incorrectly recorded data, discussed any interesting or surprising bird detections, and completed a Transect Visit Log summarizing the day's efforts.

Data Entry and Validation

Our protocol requires crews working at each large park to enter their own data into the project database throughout the field season. The crew worked three additional days at the end of the field season to continue entering and verifying data. Subsequent to the field season, the Field Lead spent an additional 16 days entering and verifying the remaining data, processing photos, and scanning data forms. Data entry procedures followed the guidelines in Siegel et al. (2010).

The database includes built-in quality assurance components such as pick-lists and validation rules to test for missing data or illogical combinations. While entering the data, the data entry person visually reviewed her or his work to ensure that the data on the screen matched the field form. When all the data were entered, we inspected the database for incompleteness and errors, and used the built-in Quality Assurance Tools to check for logical inconsistencies and data outliers. Any errors or data omissions were then corrected.

Data Analysis

We summarized and tabulated data according to the template in Siegel et al. (2010). We present survey results without making any adjustments for detectability, which may vary substantially by species, habitat, observer, or other factors. In conjunction with periodic trend analyses for this monitoring project, factors affecting detectability of birds during point counts will be assessed quantitatively, allowing for annual results to be adjusted to account for variable detectability (Buckland et al. 2001). Until that analysis is completed, any results should be viewed as provisional only.

Results

Of the 15 annual-panel transects in each large park, we surveyed 13 transects in SEKI and 13 transects in YOSE (Table 2). Of the 15 transects in the first alternating panel at each park, we surveyed 11 transects at SEKI and 14 transects at YOSE (Table 2). A total of 51 transects were surveyed at SEKI and YOSE, and the numbers completed by park and elevation category are indicated in Table 3. We conducted 360 individual point counts at SEKI and 384 point counts at YOSE (Table 2). We also conducted 42 point counts at DEPO. During the 744 point counts in the two large parks, we counted 6,507 individual birds. Across the two large parks, we documented the presence of 121 species (Table 4), 96 of which were detected during point counts; the remaining 25 species were recorded only as incidental detections or on "Rare Bird Report Forms".

For the annual-panel transects only, the number of individuals of each species detected during point counts (unlimited radius) and the number of transects on which each species was detected are provided in Table 5. On the annual-panel transects, we detected 79 bird species during point counts at SEKI and 75 species during point counts at YOSE (Table 5). Pooling detections on annual-panel transects across all species, we amassed 1,964 individual bird detections (9.97 detections/point; n = 197 points; SE = 0.43) at SEKI and 1,467 detections (8.10 detections per point; n = 181 points; SE = 0.38) at YOSE (Table 5). The five most frequently detected species on the annual-panel transects in 2011 were: dark-eyed junco (290 detections), mountain chickadee (217 detections), Steller's jay (187 detections), yellow-rumped warbler (178 detections), and western tanager (143 detections).

Pooling data across the annual-panel transects as well as the transects in the first alternating panel ("Alt2"), the number of individuals of each species detected during point counts (unlimited radius) and the number of transects on which each species was detected are provided in Table 6. Using data pooled across all transects, we detected 82 bird species during point counts at SEKI and 87 species during point counts at YOSE (Table 6). Considering data from all 51 surveyed transects, the five most frequently detected species were: dark-eyed junco (569 detections), mountain chickadee (470 detections), yellow-rumped warbler (403 detections), Steller's jay (357 detections), and red-breasted nuthatch (285 detections).

Two species of particular conservation interest—bald eagle (formerly a federally endangered species) and black-backed woodpecker (currently a candidate species for listing as threatened or endangered in California)—were detected at times other than during point counts, and were documented on "Rare Bird Report Forms". Rare Bird Reports of these species (not including point count detections, which are documented in Table 6) are summarized in Table 7.

For the 72 species for which we amassed at least three point count detections in 2011, we present the total number of detections of each species on each park's annual panel transects during the 2011 field season (Figure 5). These detection totals, along with those collected in future years, will be adjusted for differences in survey effort or potential differences in detectability of birds between years; such adjustments will be made in conjunction with our trend analyses, which are intended to be conducted after every fourth year of sampling.

At DEPO our 42 point counts yielded 353 detections of 42 species (Table 8), for a detection rate of 8.40 (n = 42; SE = 0.54) birds per point. The most frequently detected species was fox sparrow (52 detections), followed by western wood-pewee (32 detections), dark-eyed junco (31 detections), yellow-rumped warbler (30 detections), and mountain chickadee (23 detections).

Table 2. SIEN bird monitoring transects intended for survey in 2011, their panel assignment, elevation category, and the number of points actually surveyed along the transect in 2011. 'Ann1' indicates the annual panel. 'Alt2' indicates alternating panel 2, the first of four alternating panels to be surveyed. An entry of 0 in "No. of points surveyed" indicates the crew was not able to visit the transect.

Park	Panel	Elevation	Transect	No. of points surveyed
SEKI	Ann1	Low	8021	17
SEKI	Ann1	Medium	8001	21
SEKI	Ann1	Medium	8002	14
SEKI	Ann1	Medium	8005	12
SEKI	Ann1	Medium	8006	14
SEKI	Ann1	Medium	8008	11
SEKI	Ann1	Medium	8010	15
SEKI	Ann1	Medium	8013	13
SEKI	Ann1	Medium	8017	10
SEKI	Ann1	Medium	8100	20
SEKI	Ann1	High	8003	19
SEKI	Ann1	High	8004	18
SEKI	Ann1	High	8007	13
SEKI	Ann1	High	8011	0
SEKI	Ann1	High	8012	0
SEKI	Alt2	Low	8034	15
SEKI	Alt2	Medium	8022	13
SEKI	Alt2	Medium	8024	0
SEKI	Alt2	Medium	8025	14
SEKI	Alt2	Medium	8029	15
SEKI	Alt2	Medium	8030	0
SEKI	Alt2	Medium	8032	14
SEKI	Alt2	Medium	8033	14
SEKI	Alt2	Medium	8035	18
SEKI	Alt2	Medium	8102	0
SEKI	Alt2	High	8014	16
SEKI	Alt2	High	8015	16
SEKI	Alt2	High	8016	0
SEKI	Alt2	High	8019	14
SEKI	Alt2	High	8020	14
YOSE	Ann1	Low	6015	17
YOSE	Ann1	Low	6017	13
YOSE	Ann1	Low	6022	18
YOSE	Ann1	Low	6103	11
YOSE	Ann1	Low	6107	13
YOSE	Ann1	Medium	6026	12
YOSE	Ann1	Medium	6029	11
YOSE	Ann1	Medium	6032	13

Table 2. SIEN bird monitoring transects intended for survey in 2011, their panel assignment, elevation category, and the number of points actually surveyed along the transect in 2011. 'Ann1' indicates the annual panel. 'Alt2' indicates alternating panel 2, the first of four alternating panels to be surveyed. An entry of 0 in "No. of points surveyed" indicates the crew was not able to visit the transect (continued).

Park	Panel	Elevation	Transect	No. of points surveyed
YOSE	Ann1	Medium	6034	12
YOSE	Ann1	Medium	6040	0
YOSE	Ann1	High	6014	16
YOSE	Ann1	High	6016	14
YOSE	Ann1	High	6019	14
YOSE	Ann1	High	6023	17
YOSE	Ann1	High	6028	0
YOSE	Alt2	Low	6001	12
YOSE	Alt2	Low	6002	22
YOSE	Alt2	Low	6005	13
YOSE	Alt2	Low	6011	13
YOSE	Alt2	Low	6105	14
YOSE	Alt2	Medium	6009	14
YOSE	Alt2	Medium	6010	13
YOSE	Alt2	Medium	6013	0
YOSE	Alt2	Medium	6020	12
YOSE	Alt2	Medium	6024	13
YOSE	Alt2	High	6003	15
YOSE	Alt2	High	6004	17
YOSE	Alt2	High	6007	15
YOSE	Alt2	High	6008	15
YOSE	Alt2	High	6012	15

Table 3. Summary of SIEN bird monitoring transects completed through 2011.

Park	Elevation	Number of transects completed 2011[a]
SEKI	Low	2 of 2
SEKI	Medium	15 of 18
SEKI	High	7 of 10
SEKI	All	24 of 30
YOSE	Low	10 of 10
YOSE	Medium	8 of 10
YOSE	High	9 of 10
YOSE	All	27 of 30
ALL	Low	12 of 12
ALL	Medium	23 of 28
ALL	High	16 of 20
ALL	All	51 of 60

[a] The annual panel along with the first alternating panel were surveyed in 2011.

Table 4. All species recorded in SEKI and YOSE during the 2011 field season, including the pre-season training session. Columns for each park indicate the detection method, where 'Point Count' indicates species detected during point counts regardless of whether they were also recorded as rare birds or incidental detections in the same park, and 'Rare Bird' indicates species recorded on rare bird forms, regardless of whether they were also recorded as incidental detections. Species in this and subsequent tables are sorted in taxonomic order (AOU 1998).

Common Name	Scientific Name	SEKI	YOSE
Canada Goose	Branta canadensis		Point Count
Mallard	Anas platyrhynchos	Incidental	Point Count
Common Merganser	Mergus merganser		Point Count
Mountain Quail	Oreortyx pictus	Point Count	Point Count
California Quail	Callipepla californica	Point Count	Point Count
Sooty Grouse	Dendragapus fuliginosus	Point Count	Point Count
Turkey Vulture	Cathartes aura	Incidental	
Bald Eagle	Haliaeetus leucocephalus		Rare Bird
Sharp-shinned Hawk	Accipiter striatus	Point Count	
Cooper's Hawk	Accipiter cooperii	Incidental	
Northern Goshawk	Accipiter gentilis	Point Count	Point Count
Red-shouldered Hawk	Buteo lineatus	Point Count	
Red-tailed Hawk	Buteo jamaicensis	Point Count	Incidental
Golden Eagle	Aquila chrysaetos		Incidental
American Kestrel	Falco sparverius	Incidental	Point Count
Prairie Falcon	Falco mexicanus	Rare Bird	
Spotted Sandpiper	Actitis macularius		Point Count
California Gull	Larus californicus		Incidental
Band-tailed Pigeon	Patagioenas fasciata	Point Count	Incidental
Mourning Dove	Zenaida macroura	Incidental	Point Count
Northern Pygmy-Owl	Glaucidium gnoma	Incidental	
Common Nighthawk	Chordeiles minor	Point Count	
Common Poorwill	Phalaenoptilus nuttallii		Incidental
Vaux's Swift	Chaetura vauxi	Incidental	Incidental
White-throated Swift	Aeronautes saxatalis	Point Count	Point Count
Anna's Hummingbird	Calypte anna	Incidental	Point Count
Calliope Hummingbird	Stellula calliope	Point Count	Point Count
Rufous Hummingbird	Selasphorus rufus	Point Count	Incidental
Acorn Woodpecker	Melanerpes formicivorus	Point Count	Point Count
Williamson's Sapsucker	Sphyrapicus thyroideus	Point Count	Point Count
Red-breasted Sapsucker	Sphyrapicus ruber	Point Count	Point Count
Nuttall's Woodpecker	Picoides nuttallii	Point Count	
Downy Woodpecker	Picoides pubescens	Point Count	Point Count
Hairy Woodpecker	Picoides villosus	Point Count	Point Count
White-headed Woodpecker	Picoides albolarvatus	Point Count	Point Count
Black-backed Woodpecker	Picoides arcticus		Rare Bird

Table 4. All species recorded in SEKI and YOSE during the 2011 field season, including the pre-season training session. Columns for each park indicate the detection method, where 'Point Count' indicates species detected during point counts regardless of whether they were also recorded as rare birds or incidental detections in the same park, and 'Rare Bird' indicates species recorded on rare bird forms, regardless of whether they were also recorded as incidental detections. Species in this and subsequent tables are sorted in taxonomic order (AOU 1998) (continued).

Common Name	Scientific Name	SEKI	YOSE
Northern Flicker	*Colaptes auratus*	Point Count	Point Count
Pileated Woodpecker	*Dryocopus pileatus*	Point Count	Point Count
Olive-sided Flycatcher	*Contopus cooperi*	Point Count	Point Count
Western Wood-Pewee	*Contopus sordidulus*	Point Count	Point Count
Hammond's Flycatcher	*Empidonax hammondii*	Point Count	Point Count
Gray Flycatcher	*Empidonax wrightii*		Rare Bird
Dusky Flycatcher	*Empidonax oberholseri*	Point Count	Point Count
Pacific-slope Flycatcher	*Empidonax difficilis*	Point Count	Point Count
Black Phoebe	*Sayornis nigricans*	Incidental	Incidental
Say's Phoebe	*Sayornis saya*		Point Count
Ash-throated Flycatcher	*Myiarchus cinerascens*	Point Count	Incidental
Western Kingbird	*Tyrannus verticalis*		Incidental
Cassin's Vireo	*Vireo cassinii*	Point Count	Point Count
Hutton's Vireo	*Vireo huttoni*	Incidental	Point Count
Warbling Vireo	*Vireo gilvus*	Point Count	Point Count
Steller's Jay	*Cyanocitta stelleri*	Point Count	Point Count
Western Scrub-Jay	*Aphelocoma californica*	Point Count	Point Count
Clark's Nutcracker	*Nucifraga columbiana*	Point Count	Point Count
Common Raven	*Corvus corax*	Point Count	Point Count
Horned Lark	*Eremophila alpestris*		Incidental
Northern Rough-winged Swallow	*Stelgidopteryx serripennis*	Incidental	Incidental
Cliff Swallow	*Petrochelidon pyrrhonota*	Incidental	Point Count
Mountain Chickadee	*Poecile gambeli*	Point Count	Point Count
Oak Titmouse	*Baeolophus inornatus*	Point Count	Point Count
Bushtit	*Psaltriparus minimus*	Point Count	Point Count
Red-breasted Nuthatch	*Sitta canadensis*	Point Count	Point Count
White-breasted Nuthatch	*Sitta carolinensis*	Point Count	Point Count
Brown Creeper	*Certhia americana*	Point Count	Point Count
Rock Wren	*Salpinctes obsoletus*	Point Count	Point Count
Canyon Wren	*Catherpes mexicanus*	Point Count	Point Count
Bewick's Wren	*Thryomanes bewickii*	Point Count	Point Count
House Wren	*Troglodytes aedon*	Point Count	Point Count
Pacific Wren	*Troglodytes pacificus*	Point Count	Point Count
Blue-gray Gnatcatcher	*Polioptila caerulea*	Point Count	Point Count
American Dipper	*Cinclus mexicanus*	Incidental	Incidental
Golden-crowned Kinglet	*Regulus satrapa*	Point Count	Point Count
Ruby-crowned Kinglet	*Regulus calendula*	Point Count	Point Count

Table 4. All species recorded in SEKI and YOSE during the 2011 field season, including the pre-season training session. Columns for each park indicate the detection method, where 'Point Count' indicates species detected during point counts regardless of whether they were also recorded as rare birds or incidental detections in the same park, and 'Rare Bird' indicates species recorded on rare bird forms, regardless of whether they were also recorded as incidental detections. Species in this and subsequent tables are sorted in taxonomic order (AOU 1998) (continued).

Common Name	Scientific Name	SEKI	YOSE
Wrentit	*Chamaea fasciata*	Point Count	Point Count
Western Bluebird	*Sialia mexicana*	Point Count	Point Count
Mountain Bluebird	*Sialia currucoides*	Point Count	Point Count
Townsend's Solitaire	*Myadestes townsendi*	Point Count	Point Count
Hermit Thrush	*Catharus guttatus*	Point Count	Point Count
American Robin	*Turdus migratorius*	Point Count	Point Count
California Thrasher	*Toxostoma redivivum*	Incidental	Incidental
European Starling	*Sturnus vulgaris*	Incidental	Incidental
American Pipit	*Anthus rubescens*	Point Count	Point Count
Orange-crowned Warbler	*Oreothlypis celata*	Point Count	Point Count
Nashville Warbler	*Oreothlypis ruficapilla*	Point Count	Point Count
MacGillivray's Warbler	*Geothlypis tolmiei*	Point Count	Point Count
Yellow Warbler	*Setophaga petechia*	Point Count	Point Count
Yellow-rumped Warbler	*Setophaga coronata*	Point Count	Point Count
Black-throated Gray Warbler	*Setophaga nigrescens*	Point Count	Point Count
Townsend's Warbler	*Setophaga townsendi*		Incidental
Hermit Warbler	*Setophaga occidentalis*	Point Count	Point Count
Wilson's Warbler	*Cardellina pusilla*	Point Count	Point Count
Green-tailed Towhee	*Pipilo chlorurus*	Point Count	Point Count
Spotted Towhee	*Pipilo maculatus*	Point Count	Point Count
California Towhee	*Melozone crissalis*	Point Count	Point Count
Chipping Sparrow	*Spizella passerina*	Point Count	Point Count
Brewer's Sparrow	*Spizella breweri*	Point Count	Rare Bird
Fox Sparrow	*Passerella iliaca*	Point Count	Point Count
Song Sparrow	*Melospiza melodia*	Point Count	Point Count
Lincoln's Sparrow	*Melospiza lincolnii*	Point Count	Point Count
White-crowned Sparrow	*Zonotrichia leucophrys*	Point Count	Point Count
Golden-crowned Sparrow	*Zonotrichia atricapilla*	Point Count	Incidental
Dark-eyed Junco	*Junco hyemalis*	Point Count	Point Count
Western Tanager	*Piranga ludoviciana*	Point Count	Point Count
Black-headed Grosbeak	*Pheucticus melanocephalus*	Point Count	Point Count
Lazuli Bunting	*Passerina amoena*	Point Count	Point Count
Red-winged Blackbird	*Agelaius phoeniceus*		Point Count
Brewer's Blackbird	*Euphagus cyanocephalus*	Point Count	Point Count
Brown-headed Cowbird	*Molothrus ater*	Point Count	Point Count
Bullock's Oriole	*Icterus bullockii*		Incidental

Table 4. All species recorded in SEKI and YOSE during the 2011 field season, including the pre-season training session. Columns for each park indicate the detection method, where 'Point Count' indicates species detected during point counts regardless of whether they were also recorded as rare birds or incidental detections in the same park, and 'Rare Bird' indicates species recorded on rare bird forms, regardless of whether they were also recorded as incidental detections. Species in this and subsequent tables are sorted in taxonomic order (AOU 1998) (continued).

Common Name	Scientific Name	SEKI	YOSE
Gray-crowned Rosy-Finch	*Leucosticte tephrocotis*	Point Count	Point Count
Pine Grosbeak	*Pinicola enucleator*	Incidental	Point Count
Purple Finch	*Carpodacus purpureus*	Point Count	Point Count
Cassin's Finch	*Carpodacus cassinii*	Point Count	Point Count
House Finch	*Carpodacus mexicanus*	Incidental	
Red Crossbill	*Loxia curvirostra*	Point Count	Incidental
Pine Siskin	*Spinus pinus*	Point Count	Point Count
Lesser Goldfinch	*Spinus psaltria*	Point Count	Point Count
Evening Grosbeak	*Coccothraustes vespertinus*	Point Count	Point Count

Table 5. Number of transects with detections and number of individual detections for each species detected during point counts on annual-panel transects in SEKI and YOSE in 2011.

Species	Number of transects with detections			Number of individual detections		
	SEKI	YOSE	ALL	SEKI	YOSE	ALL
Mountain Quail	8	7	15	82	51	133
California Quail	1	1	2	5	1	6
Sooty Grouse	2	1	3	3	1	4
Northern Goshawk	1	1	2	1	1	2
Red-shouldered Hawk	1		1	1		1
Red-tailed Hawk	1		1	1		1
American Kestrel		1	1		1	1
Spotted Sandpiper		2	2		6	6
Band-tailed Pigeon	2		2	2		2
Mourning Dove		1	1		3	3
White-throated Swift	2	2	4	4	7	11
Anna's Hummingbird		4	4		6	6
Calliope Hummingbird	1		1	2		2
Rufous Hummingbird	2		2	2		2
Acorn Woodpecker	3	4	7	4	18	22
Williamson's Sapsucker	2	1	3	3	1	4
Red-breasted Sapsucker	7	3	10	9	5	14
Nuttall's Woodpecker	1		1	1		1
Hairy Woodpecker	3	7	10	5	12	17
White-headed Woodpecker	6	6	12	20	12	32
Northern Flicker	10	10	20	23	31	54
Pileated Woodpecker	2	2	4	6	7	13
Olive-sided Flycatcher	7	4	11	29	12	41
Western Wood-Pewee	9	7	16	64	58	122
Hammond's Flycatcher	4	4	8	16	6	22
Dusky Flycatcher	11	10	21	39	72	111
Pacific-slope Flycatcher	4	2	6	11	4	15

Table 5. Number of transects with detections and number of individual detections for each species detected during point counts on annual-panel transects in SEKI and YOSE in 2011 (continued).

Species	Number of transects with detections			Number of individual detections		
	SEKI	YOSE	ALL	SEKI	YOSE	ALL
Say's Phoebe		1	1		1	1
Ash-throated Flycatcher	1		1	5		5
Cassin's Vireo	3	6	9	10	26	36
Hutton's Vireo		1	1		1	1
Warbling Vireo	8	6	14	20	20	40
Steller's Jay	10	9	19	108	79	187
Western Scrub-Jay	2	2	4	13	8	21
Clark's Nutcracker	5	5	10	34	23	57
Common Raven	5	3	8	7	10	17
Mountain Chickadee	12	12	24	147	70	217
Oak Titmouse	1		1	7		7
Bushtit	1	1	2	1	1	2
Red-breasted Nuthatch	8	8	16	114	25	139
White-breasted Nuthatch	4	2	6	7	3	10
Brown Creeper	10	9	19	54	31	85
Rock Wren	2	1	3	3	1	4
Canyon Wren	2	4	6	2	7	9
Bewick's Wren	2	3	5	6	3	9
House Wren	1	2	3	1	12	13
Pacific Wren	2		2	3		3
Blue-gray Gnatcatcher	3	3	6	5	7	12
Golden-crowned Kinglet	6	6	12	78	17	95
Ruby-crowned Kinglet	1	3	4	1	6	7
Wrentit	3	2	5	35	10	45
Western Bluebird	1	1	2	1	2	3
Mountain Bluebird	1	1	2	11	3	14
Townsend's Solitaire	8	6	14	21	13	34

Table 5. Number of transects with detections and number of individual detections for each species detected during point counts on annual-panel transects in SEKI and YOSE in 2011 (continued).

Species	Number of transects with detections			Number of individual detections		
	SEKI	YOSE	ALL	SEKI	YOSE	ALL
Hermit Thrush	6	6	12	19	25	44
American Robin	9	9	18	61	48	109
American Pipit	1	1	2	1	2	3
Orange-crowned Warbler	2		2	15		15
Nashville Warbler	7	7	14	63	54	117
MacGillivray's Warbler	8	8	16	28	29	57
Yellow Warbler	2	2	4	3	7	10
Yellow-rumped Warbler	13	13	26	98	80	178
Black-throated Gray Warbler	2	4	6	11	11	22
Hermit Warbler	5	6	11	24	35	59
Wilson's Warbler	4	6	10	9	19	28
Green-tailed Towhee	1	1	2	1	3	4
Spotted Towhee	5	5	10	58	43	101
California Towhee	1	1	2	6	1	7
Chipping Sparrow	2	5	7	2	7	9
Fox Sparrow	9	5	14	87	53	140
Song Sparrow	3	3	6	8	14	22
Lincoln's Sparrow	3	5	8	10	8	18
White-crowned Sparrow	2	5	7	7	20	27
Dark-eyed Junco	12	13	25	158	132	290
Western Tanager	9	8	17	93	50	143
Black-headed Grosbeak	4	6	10	41	32	73
Lazuli Bunting	2	2	4	2	3	5
Red-winged Blackbird		2	2		12	12
Brewer's Blackbird	1	1	2	6	6	12
Brown-headed Cowbird	1	3	4	1	11	12
Gray-crowned Rosy-Finch	4	1	5	61	1	62

Table 5. Number of transects with detections and number of individual detections for each species detected during point counts on annual-panel transects in SEKI and YOSE in 2011 (continued).

| Species | Number of transects with detections | | | Number of individual detections | | |
	SEKI	YOSE	ALL	SEKI	YOSE	ALL
Purple Finch	7	2	9	21	2	23
Cassin's Finch	10	8	18	22	44	66
Pine Siskin	6	5	11	14	20	34
Lesser Goldfinch	1	1	2	4	1	5
Evening Grosbeak	2	2	2	3		3
All species pooled				1,964	1,467	3,431
Ave. detections (all species pooled) per point (n, SE)				9.97 (197, 0.43)	8.10(181, 0.38)	9.08 (378, 0.92)

Table 6. Number of transects with detections and number of individual detections for each species detected during point counts (annual- and alternating-panel transects combined) in SEKI and YOSE in 2011.

Species	Number of transects with detections			Number of individual detections		
	SEKI	YOSE	ALL	SEKI	YOSE	ALL
Canada Goose		1	1		1	1
Mallard		1	1		2	2
Common Merganser		1	1		4	4
Mountain Quail	12	14	26	118	80	198
California Quail	1	1	2	5	1	6
Sooty Grouse	5	3	8	8	4	12
Sharp-shinned Hawk	2		2	2		2
Northern Goshawk	1	1	2	1	1	2
Red-shouldered Hawk	1		1	1		1
Red-tailed Hawk	1		1	1		1
American Kestrel		1	1		1	1
Spotted Sandpiper		3	3		7	7
Band-tailed Pigeon	3		3	3		3
Mourning Dove		1	1		3	3
Common Nighthawk	1		1	3		3
White-throated Swift	2	5	7	4	37	41
Anna's Hummingbird		7	7		11	11
Calliope Hummingbird	3	1	4	4	1	5
Rufous Hummingbird	3		3	4		4
Acorn Woodpecker	3	6	9	4	37	41
Williamson's Sapsucker	5	5	10	7	10	17
Red-breasted Sapsucker	12	6	18	15	9	24
Nuttall's Woodpecker	1		1	1		1
Downy Woodpecker		1	1		1	1
Hairy Woodpecker	8	15	23	13	22	35
White-headed Woodpecker	9	10	19	27	27	54
Northern Flicker	17	19	36	41	60	101

23

Table 6. Number of transects with detections and number of individual detections for each species detected during point counts (annual- and alternating-panel transects combined) in in SEKI and YOSE in 2011 (continued).

Species	Number of transects with detections			Number of individual detections		
	SEKI	YOSE	ALL	SEKI	YOSE	ALL
Pileated Woodpecker	5	6	11	16	17	33
Olive-sided Flycatcher	11	11	22	38	37	75
Western Wood-Pewee	17	16	33	113	107	220
Hammond's Flycatcher	11	7	18	32	15	47
Dusky Flycatcher	20	21	41	83	134	217
Pacific-slope Flycatcher	6	5	11	17	8	25
Say's Phoebe	1	1	1		1	1
Ash-throated Flycatcher	1		1	5		5
Cassin's Vireo	4	12	16	15	52	67
Hutton's Vireo	2	2	2		2	2
Warbling Vireo	12	13	25	36	49	85
Steller's Jay	17	21	38	167	190	357
Western Scrub-Jay	2	3	5	13	9	22
Clark's Nutcracker	10	11	21	59	51	110
Common Raven	8	9	17	19	24	43
Northern Rough-winged Swallow	1	1	1		1	1
Mountain Chickadee	23	26	49	276	194	470
Oak Titmouse	1	1	2	7	1	8
Bushtit	1	3	4	1	7	8
Red-breasted Nuthatch	14	20	34	190	96	286
White-breasted Nuthatch	6	3	9	10	4	14
Brown Creeper	19	20	39	83	66	149
Rock Wren	2	2	4	3	2	5
Canyon Wren	3	5	8	3	12	15
Bewick's Wren	2	4	6	6	4	10
House Wren	1	3	4	1	14	15
Pacific Wren	6	2	8	7	4	11

24

Table 6. Number of transects with detections and number of individual detections for each species detected during point counts (annual- and alternating-panel transects combined) in SEKI and YOSE in 2011 (continued).

Species	Number of transects with detections			Number of individual detections		
	SEKI	YOSE	ALL	SEKI	YOSE	ALL
Blue-gray Gnatcatcher	3	3	6	5	7	12
Golden-crowned Kinglet	12	13	25	136	61	197
Ruby-crowned Kinglet	3	5	8	15	10	25
Wrentit	3	3	6	35	13	48
Western Bluebird	1	1	2	1	2	3
Mountain Bluebird	2	2	4	14	4	18
Townsend's Solitaire	14	14	28	30	32	62
Hermit Thrush	15	12	27	70	44	114
American Robin	18	19	37	99	113	212
American Pipit	2	3	5	7	4	11
Orange-crowned Warbler	2	1	3	15	2	17
Nashville Warbler	11	13	24	82	87	169
MacGillivray's Warbler	11	16	27	35	46	81
Yellow Warbler	4	4	8	6	10	16
Yellow-rumped Warbler	24	26	50	200	203	403
Black-throated Gray Warbler	2	6	8	11	26	37
Hermit Warbler	9	13	22	68	108	176
Wilson's Warbler	7	7	14	15	20	35
Green-tailed Towhee	1	3	4	1	12	13
Spotted Towhee	6	9	15	60	73	133
California Towhee	1	1	2	6	1	7
Chipping Sparrow	2	6	8	2	9	11
Fox Sparrow	15	14	29	137	108	245
Song Sparrow	3	4	7	8	29	37
Lincoln's Sparrow	6	9	15	17	15	32
White-crowned Sparrow	6	8	14	24	38	62
Dark-eyed Junco	23	27	50	278	291	569

Table 6. Number of transects with detections and number of individual detections for each species detected during point counts (annual- and alternating-panel transects combined) in SEKI and YOSE in 2011 (continued).

Species	Number of transects with detections			Number of individual detections		
	SEKI	YOSE	ALL	SEKI	YOSE	ALL
Western Tanager	15	17	32	132	126	258
Black-headed Grosbeak	6	11	17	54	89	143
Lazuli Bunting	2	2	4	2	3	5
Red-winged Blackbird		4	4		30	30
Brewer's Blackbird	2	2	4	47	9	56
Brown-headed Cowbird	2	5	7	3	18	21
Gray-crowned Rosy-Finch	7	2	9	70	6	76
Pine Grosbeak		3	3		5	5
Purple Finch	13	6	19	40	14	54
Cassin's Finch	18	17	35	44	81	125
Red Crossbill	3		3	6		6
Pine Siskin	11	15	26	42	45	87
Lesser Goldfinch	1	1	2	4	1	5
Evening Grosbeak	4	1	5	8	1	9
All species pooled				3,291	3,216	6,507
Detections (all species pooled) per point (n, SE)				9.14 (360, 0.33)	8.38 (384, 0.27)	8.75 (744, 0.21)
Number of species detected during point counts				82	87	96

Table 7. Species of potential management concern recorded in each park in 2011.

Species	Number of individual birds detected (during point counts, as rare birds, or as incidental observations)	
	SEKI	YOSE
Bald Eagle	0	3
Northern Goshawk	2	2
Golden Eagle	0	1
Vaux's Swift	1	1
Black-backed Woodpecker	0	4
Olive-sided Flycatcher	34	31
Yellow Warbler	5	9

Table 8. Number of points with detections and number of individual detections for each species detected during point counts at DEPO in 2011.

Species	Number of points with detections	Number of individual detections
Mountain Quail	10	13
Spotted Sandpiper	1	1
Anna's Hummingbird	1	1
Calliope Hummingbird	1	1
Williamson's Sapsucker	1	1
Red-breasted Sapsucker	4	5
Hairy Woodpecker	6	7
White-headed Woodpecker	1	1
Northern Flicker	3	3
Olive-sided Flycatcher	13	16
Western Wood-Pewee	23	32
Dusky Flycatcher	11	12
Warbling Vireo	11	12
Steller's Jay	7	8
Clark's Nutcracker	1	2
Tree Swallow	2	4
Violet-green Swallow	1	1
Northern Rough-winged Swallow	1	2
Mountain Chickadee	18	23
Red-breasted Nuthatch	8	8
Brown Creeper	3	3
House Wren	2	2
Golden-crowned Kinglet	6	7
Mountain Bluebird	2	3
Townsend's Solitaire	1	1
Hermit Thrush	1	1
American Robin	8	10
MacGillivray's Warbler	13	18
Yellow-rumped Warbler	18	30
Wilson's Warbler	2	3
Green-tailed Towhee	2	2
Chipping Sparrow	1	1
Fox Sparrow	23	52
Song Sparrow	3	3
Lincoln's Sparrow	3	4
White-crowned Sparrow	1	1
Dark-eyed Junco	21	31
Western Tanager	8	10
Brewer's Blackbird	3	4

Table 8. Number of points with detections and number of individual detections for each species detected during point counts at DEPO in 2011 (continued).

Species	Number of points with detections	Number of individual detections
Brown-headed Cowbird	2	2
Cassin's Finch	10	10
Pine Siskin	2	2
All Species Pooled		353
Detections (all species pooled) per point (n, SE)		8.40 (42, 0.54)
Number of species detected during point counts		42

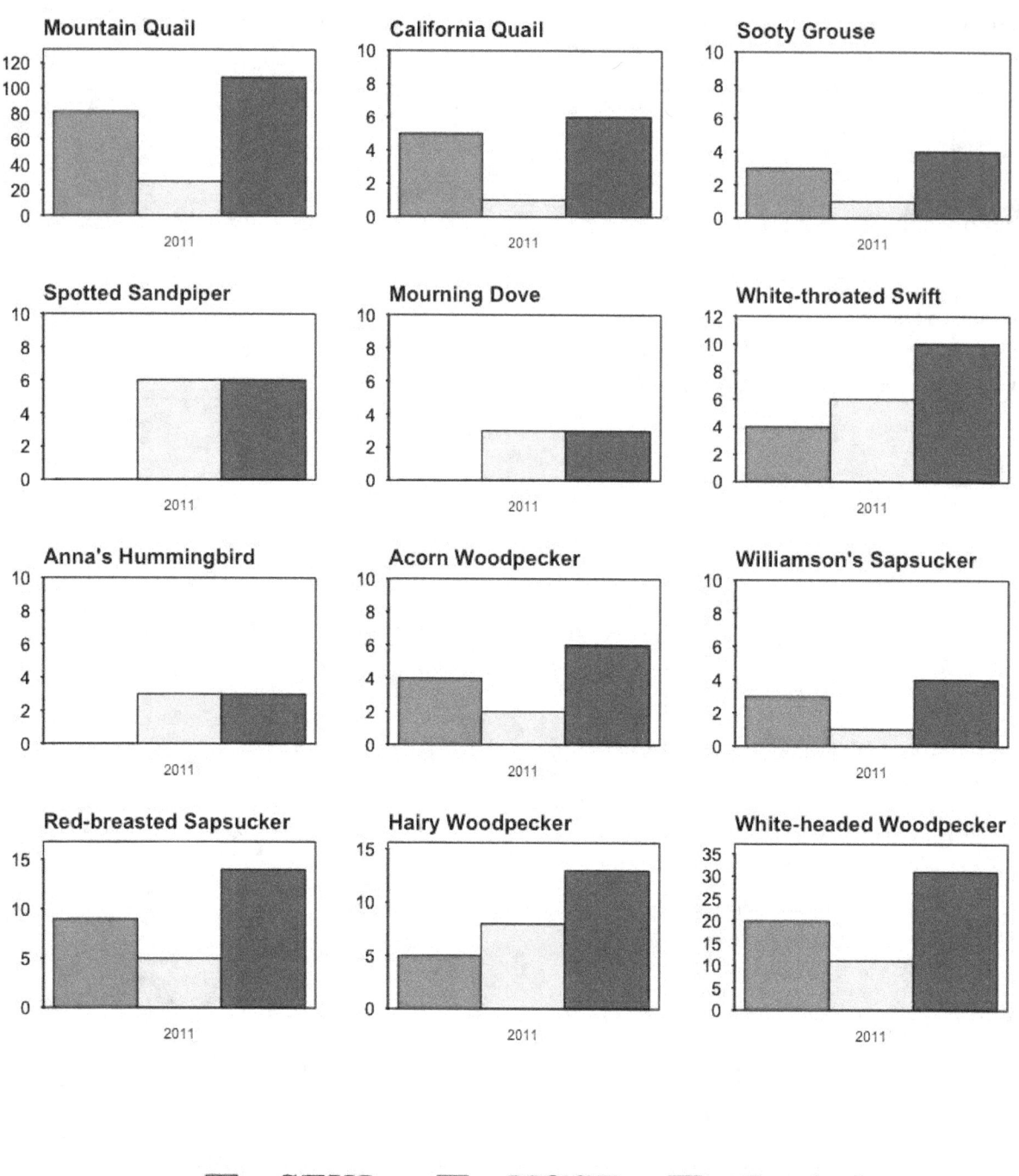

Figure 5. Number of times each species was detected on annual-panel transects at SEKI, YOSE, and both parks pooled (always presented in that order) during the 2011 field season. The figure includes all species for which we amassed at least three point count detections on annual-panel transects. These detection totals, along with those collected in future years, will be adjusted for differences in survey effort or potential differences in detectability of birds between years; such adjustments will be made in conjunction with our periodic trend analyses.

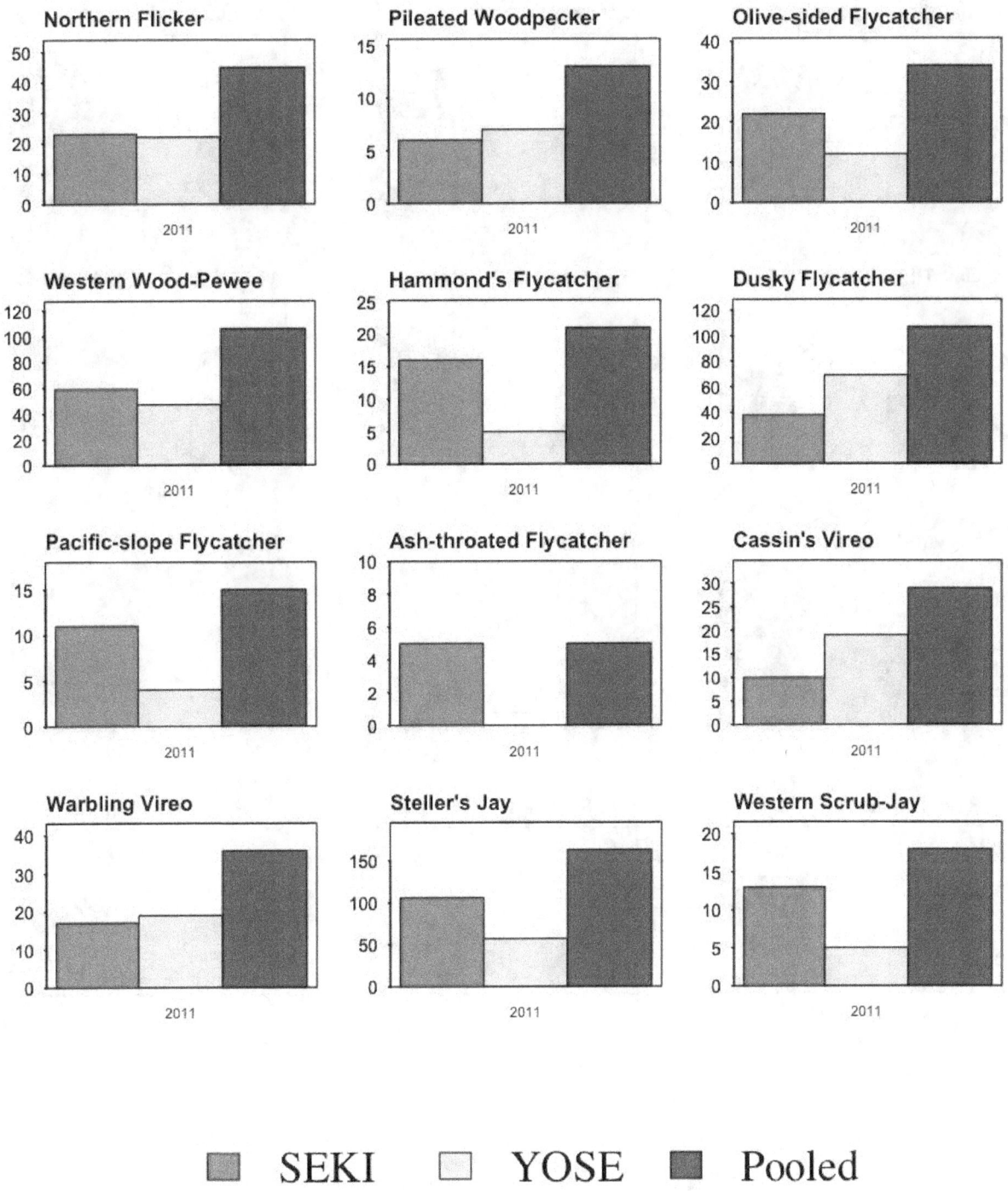

SEKI **YOSE** **Pooled**

Figure 5. Number of times each species was detected on annual-panel transects at SEKI, YOSE, and both parks pooled (always presented in that order) during the 2011 field season. The figure includes all species for which we amassed at least three point count detections on annual-panel transects. These detection totals, along with those collected in future years, will be adjusted for differences in survey effort or potential differences in detectability of birds between years; such adjustments will be made in conjunction with our periodic trend analyses (continued).

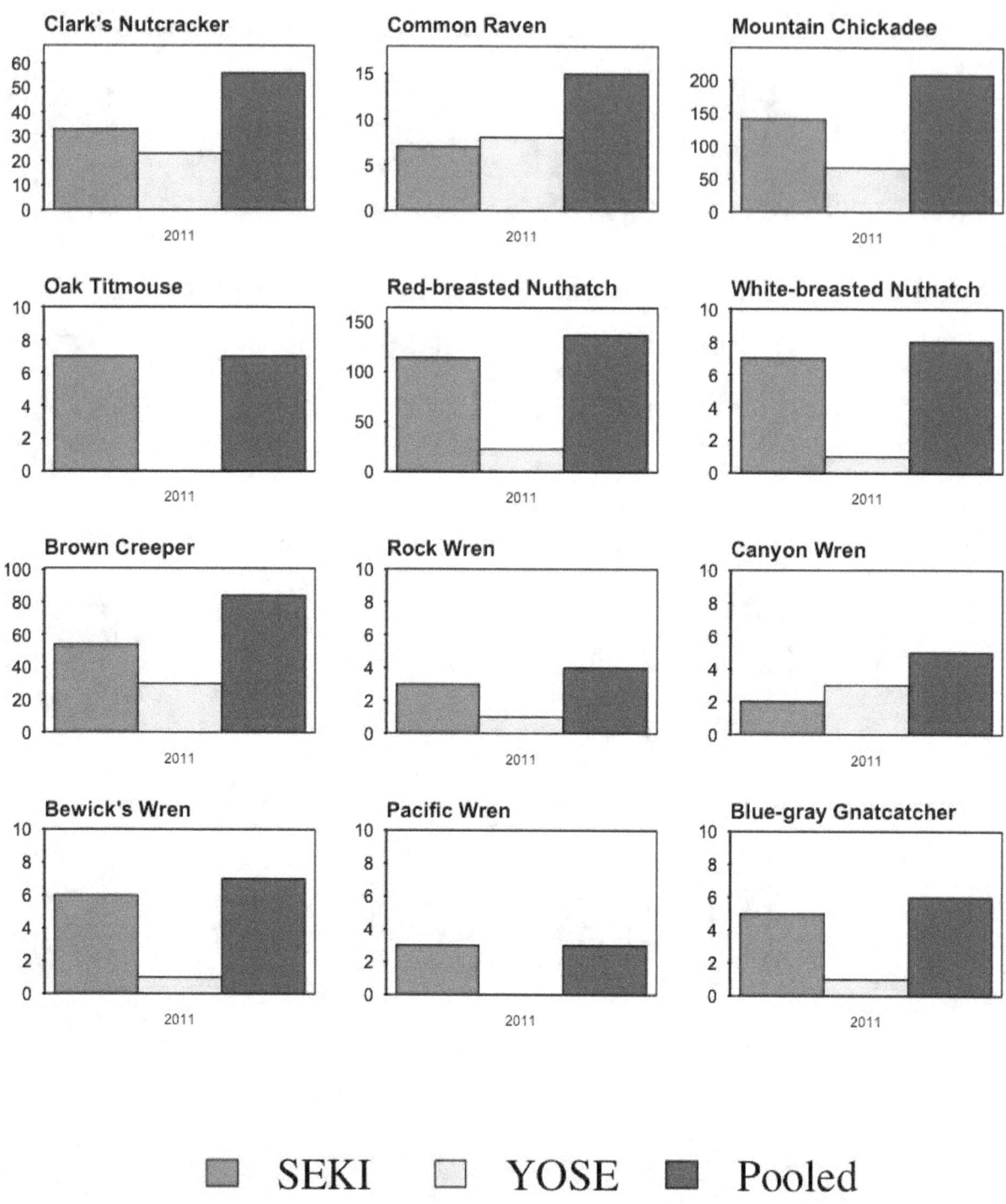

Figure 5. Number of times each species was detected on annual-panel transects at SEKI, YOSE, and both parks pooled (always presented in that order) during the 2011 field season. The figure includes all species for which we amassed at least three point count detections on annual-panel transects. These detection totals, along with those collected in future years, will be adjusted for differences in survey effort or potential differences in detectability of birds between years; such adjustments will be made in conjunction with our periodic trend analyses (continued).

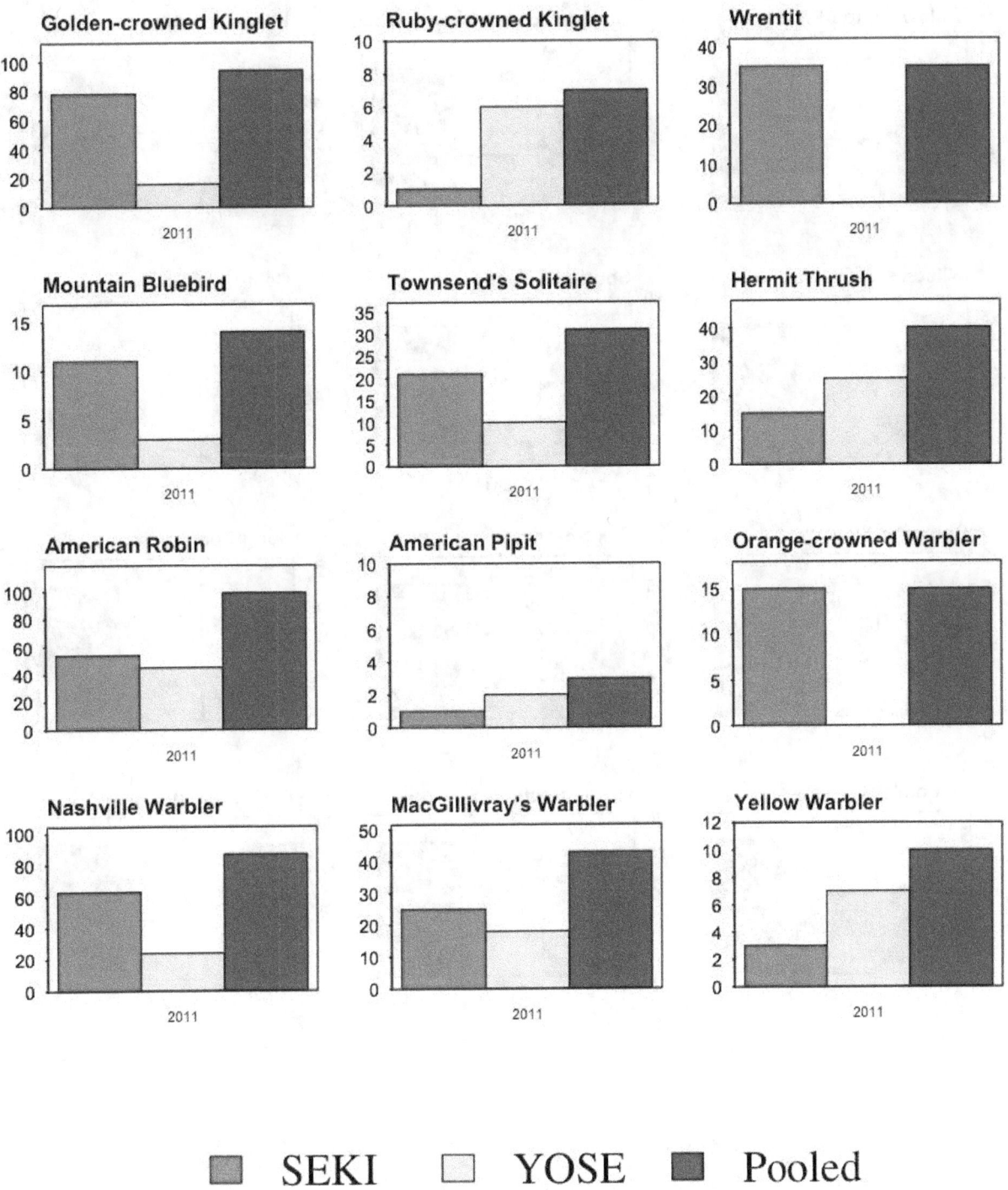

Figure 5. Number of times each species was detected on annual-panel transects at SEKI, YOSE, and both parks pooled (always presented in that order) during the 2011 field season. The figure includes all species for which we amassed at least three point count detections on annual-panel transects. These detection totals, along with those collected in future years, will be adjusted for differences in survey effort or potential differences in detectability of birds between years; such adjustments will be made in conjunction with our periodic trend analyses (continued).

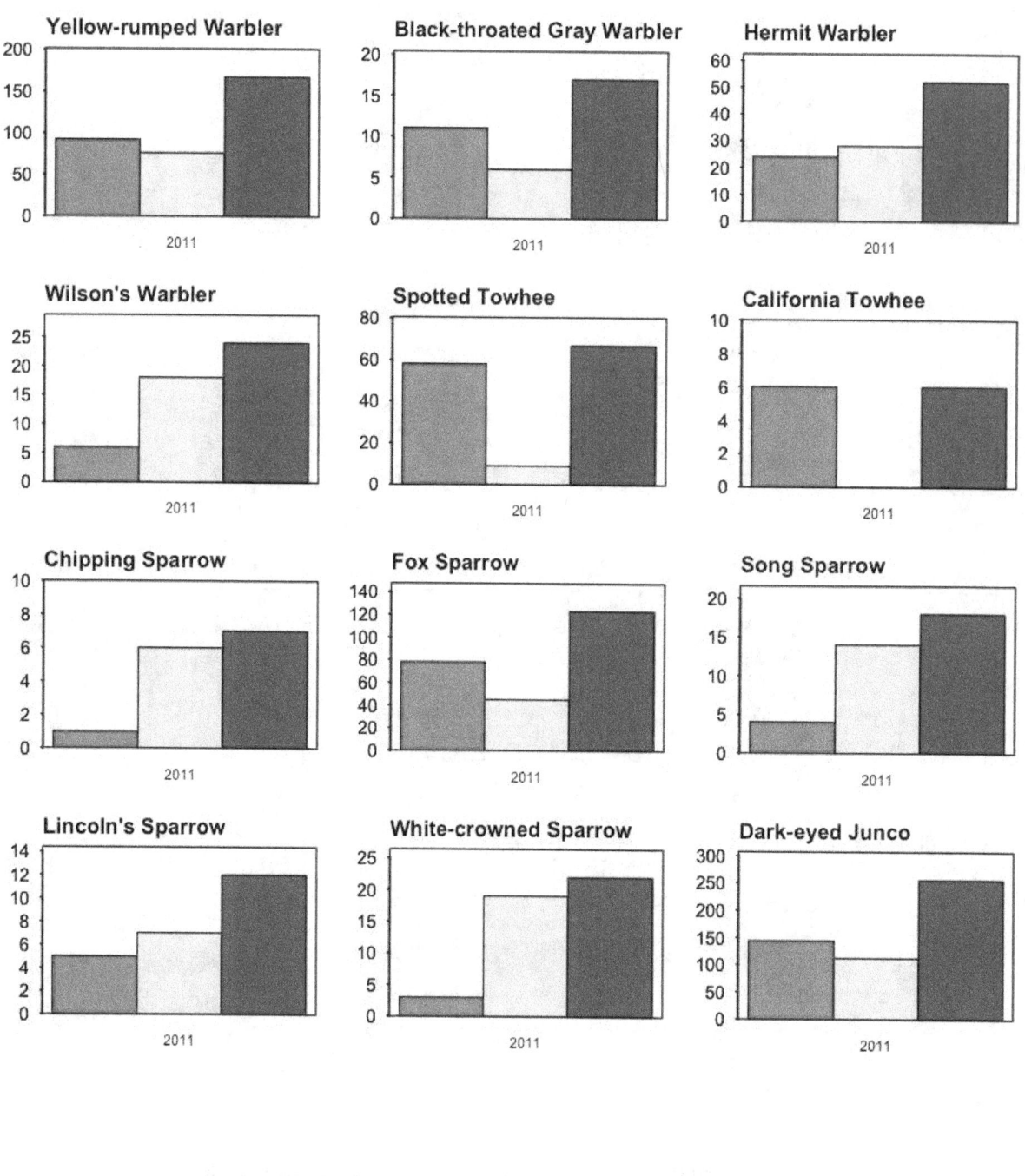

SEKI   YOSE   Pooled

Figure 5. Number of times each species was detected on annual-panel transects at SEKI, YOSE, and both parks pooled (always presented in that order) during the 2011 field season. The figure includes all species for which we amassed at least three point count detections on annual-panel transects These detection totals, along with those collected in future years, will be adjusted for differences in survey effort or potential differences in detectability of birds between years; such adjustments will be made in conjunction with our periodic trend analyses (continued).

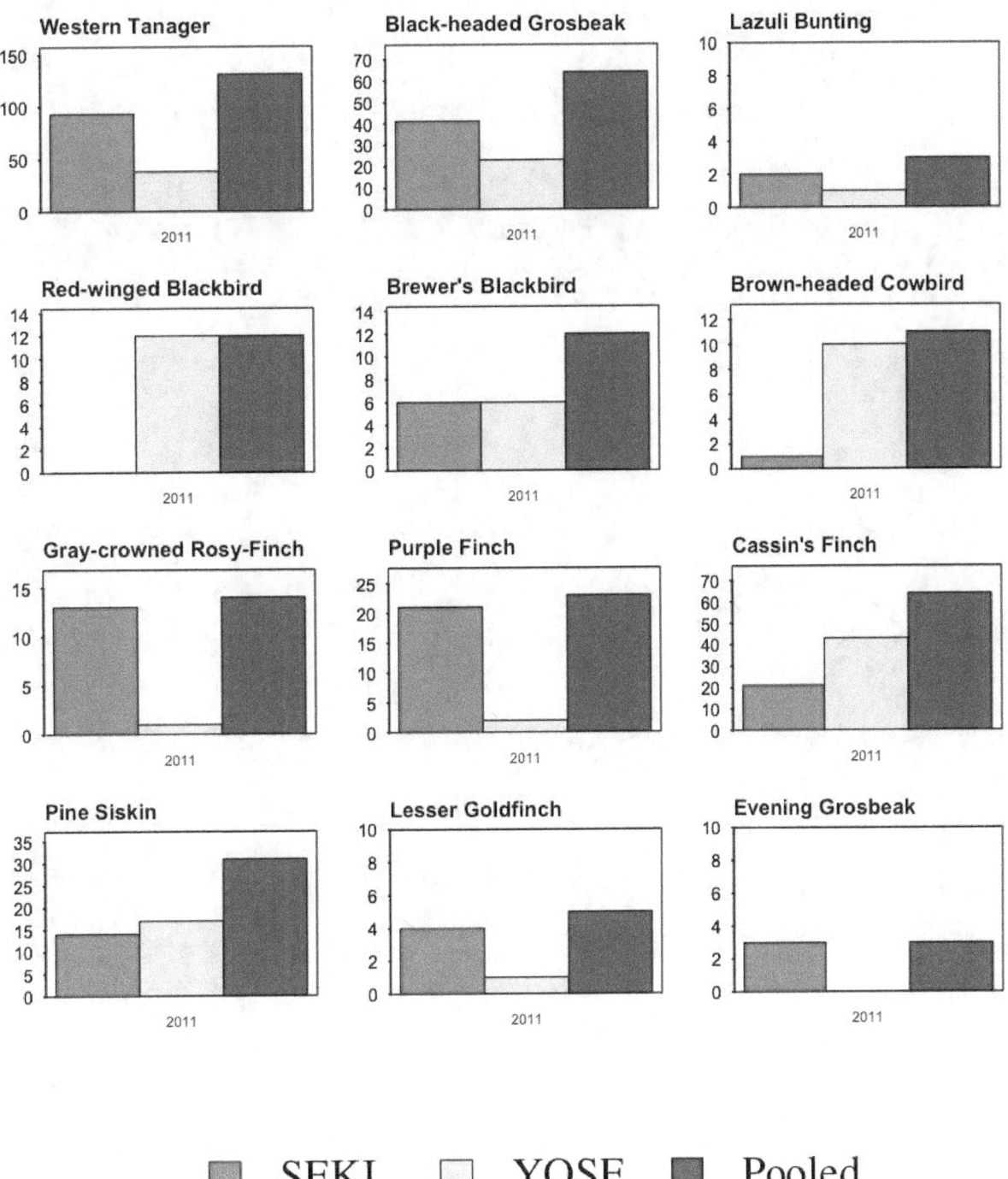

Figure 5. Number of times each species was detected on annual-panel transects at SEKI, YOSE, and both parks pooled (always presented in that order) during the 2011 field season. The figure includes all species for which we amassed at least three point count detections on annual-panel transects. These detection totals, along with those collected in future years, will be adjusted for differences in survey effort or potential differences in detectability of birds between years; such adjustments will be made in conjunction with our periodic trend analyses (continued).

Discussion

We completed our first year of full implementation long-term bird monitoring in the SIEN in 2011. Implementing the project as a partnership between SIEN personnel and IBP proceeded smoothly and efficiently, and yielded a model for collaboration that is likely to continue to serve the monitoring program well in the future.

Major challenges in 2011 were the extremely late-lingering snow across both of the large parks and high streamflows, preventing or delaying safe access to many of our middle and high-elevation transects. Although two IBP staff members and an additional IBP seasonal biologist were able to help the field crew complete some additional transects near the end of the season, the high snowpack resulted in our missing numerous transects. In the end, we were able to survey a total of 51 out of the 60 intended transects, missing four transects on the annual panel (two at SEKI and two at YOSE) and five transects on the alternating panel (four at SEKI and one at YOSE). At this writing, the 2011-2012 winter is proving to be much milder than the previous winter, and should give us the opportunity to evaluate whether surveying 60 transects plus the DEPO points is achievable under less extreme snow conditions.

Even without having surveyed all the transects, we are pleased with the high number of bird detections recorded (nearly 3,500 individual birds on annual-panel transects alone) and the relatively large number of species with tens or even hundreds of detections on those transects. These results from this first year of data collection indicate that high detection rates of common species at both SEKI and YOSE will yield a robust capacity to detect multi-year trends in bird populations. Interpreting our survey results at this juncture is premature; together with results collected in future years, they will be adjusted for differences in survey effort or potential differences in detectability of birds between years. Such adjustments will be made in conjunction with trend analyses which are to be conducted every four years (Siegel et al. 2010). With additional years of data, we will gain the capacity to assess changes in numbers of detections, to generate testable hypotheses about their causes, and to provide informed management recommendations for conserving vulnerable species.

Conclusions

In 2011, we completed the first field season of long-term bird monitoring associated with the Inventory and Monitoring Program of the SIEN. Fieldwork included data collection on the annual panel as well as the first of four alternating panels, and comprised 744 point counts at point count survey stations located along 51 transects in Sequoia and Kings Canyon National Parks (SEKI) and Yosemite National Park (YOSE), as well as 42 point count stations arrayed in a grid at Devils Postpile National Monument (DEPO). Despite particularly challenging weather conditions during this first field season of the monitoring program, preliminary results indicate we will have robust sample sizes for many species when we conduct trend analyses after additional years of data collection. Changes in bird populations that we find in subsequent years, when analyzed in the context of annual weather variation and perhaps other factors, are likely to yield interesting and useful findings about the drivers of population dynamics in birds of the Sierra Nevada, spur additional targeted research, and help refine management priorities and needs within the parks.

Literature Cited

American Ornithologists' Union (AOU). 1998. Check-list of North American birds, 7th ed. American Ornithologists' Union, Washington D.C. 829 pp.

Beedy, E. C., and S. L. Granholm. 1985. Discovering Sierra birds. Yosemite Association, El Portal, CA.

Buckland, S. T., D. R. Anderson, K. P. Burnham, J. L. Laake, D. L. Borchers, and L. Thomas. 2001. Introduction to distance sampling: estimating abundance of biological populations. Oxford University Press, Oxford, England.

DeSante, D. F., P. Pyle, and D. R. Kaschube. 2004. The 2003 annual report of the Monitoring Avian Productivity and Survivorship (MAPS) Program in Yosemite National Park. The Institute for Bird Populations, Pt. Reyes Station, CA.

DeSante, D. F., P. Pyle, and D. R. Kaschube. 2005. The Monitoring Avian Productivity and Survivorship (MAPS) Program in Sequoia and Kings Canyon and Yosemite National Parks and Devils Postpile National Monument: A comparison between time periods and locations. The Institute for Bird Populations, Pt. Reyes Station, CA.

Furness, R. W., J. J. D. Greenwood, and P. J. Jarvis. 1993. Can birds be used to monitor the environment? Pages 1–41 in R. W. Furness, and J. J. D. Greenwood, editors. Birds as monitors of environmental change. Chapman and Hall, London, England.

Gates, H. R. and S. K. Heath. 2003. Bird monitoring, habitat assessment and visitor education in montane meadow and riparian habitats of Devils Postpile National Monument: results from the 2002 and 2003 field season. PRBO Conservation Science, Stinson Beach, CA.

Greenwood, J. J. D., S. R. Baillie, H. Q. P. Crick, J. H. Marchant, and W. J. Peach. 1993. Integrated population monitoring: detecting the effects of diverse changes. Pages 267–342 in R. W. Furness and J. J. D. Greenwood, editors. Birds as monitors of environmental change. Chapman and Hall, London.

Heath, S. K. 2004. Bird monitoring in montane meadow and riparian habitats of Devils Postpile National Monument: Final report 2002–2004. Contribution #1237 of the Point Reyes Bird Observatory, Stinson Beach, CA.

Heath, S. K. 2005. Bird monitoring and education at Devils Postpile National Monument. Contribution #1304 of the Point Reyes Bird Observatory, Stinson Beach, CA.

Heath, S. K. 2007. Avian demography monitoring and visitor education at Devils Postpile National Monument, 2002–2006. Contribution #1552 of the Point Reyes Bird Observatory, Petaluma, CA.

Mayer, K. E., and J. William F. Laudenslayer. 1988. A Guide to the Wildlife Habitats of California. Page 166 in Department of Fish and Game, editor. State of California, Resources Agency, Sacramento, CA.

North American Bird Conservation Initiative, U.S. Committee. 2009. The state of the birds, United States of America, 2009. U.S. Department of Interior, Washington, DC. 36 pages.

North American Bird Conservation Initiative, U.S. Committee, 2011. The State of the Birds 2011 Report on Public Lands and Waters. U.S. Department of Interior: Washington, DC. 48 pages.

Pounds, J. A., M. P. L. Fogden, and J. H. Campbell. 1999. Biological response to climate change on a tropical mountain. Nature 398: 611-615.

Root, T. L., D. P. MacMynowski, M. D. Mastrandrea, and S. H. Schneider. 2005. Human modified temperatures induce species changes: Joint attribution. Proceedings of the National Academy of Sciences 102:7465-7469.

Root, T. L., J. T. Price, K. R. Hall, S. H. Schneider, C. Rosenzweigk, and J. A. Pounds. 2003. Fingerprints of global warming on wild animals and plants. Nature 421:57-60.

Sauer, J. R., J. E. Hines, and J. Fallon. 2008. The North American breeding bird survey, results and analysis 1966-2007. Version 5.15.2008. USGS Patuxent Wildlife Research Center, Laurel, MD.

Siegel, R. B., and D. F. DeSante. 2002. Avian inventory of Yosemite National Park (1998–2000). The Institute for Bird Populations, Point Reyes Station, CA.

Siegel, R. B., and R. L. Wilkerson. 2004. Landbird inventory for Devils Postpile National Monument. The Institute for Bird Populations, Point Reyes Station, CA.

Siegel, R. B., and R. L. Wilkerson. 2005a. Landbird inventory for Sequoia and Kings Canyon National Parks (2003–2004). The Institute for Bird Populations, Point Reyes Station, CA.

Siegel, R. B., R. L. Wilkerson, K. J. Jenkins, R. C. Kuntz II, J. R. Boetsch, J. P. Schaberl, and P. J. Happe. 2007. Landbird monitoring protocol for national parks in the North Coast and Cascades Network. U.S. Geological Survey Techniques and Methods 2-A6. U.S. Geological Survey, Reston, VA.

Siegel, R. S., P. Pyle, D. F. DeSante, and D. R. Kaschube. 2007a. The Monitoring Avian Productivity and Survivorship (MAPS) Program in Sequoia and Kings Canyon National Park: a summary of the 2006 field season, an assessment of recent trends, and a comparison with results from the MAPS Program in Yosemite National Park. The Institute for Bird Populations, Point Reyes Station, CA.

Siegel, R. B., R. L. Wilkerson, and M. Goldin Rose. 2010. Bird monitoring protocol for national parks in the Sierra Nevada Network. Natural Resource Report NPS/SIEN/NRR—2010/231. National Park Service, Fort Collins, CO.

Siegel, R. B., R. L. Wilkerson, J. F. Saracco, and Z. L. Steel. 2011. Elevation ranges of birds on the Sierra Nevada's west slope. Western Birds 42:2-26.

Silsbee, G. G., and D. L. Peterson. 1991. Designing and implementing comprehensive long-term inventory and monitoring programs for National Park System lands. Natural Resources Report NPS/NRUW/NRR-91/04, Denver, CO.

Simons, T. R., K. N. Rabenold, D. A. Buehler, J. A. Collazo, and K. E. Fransreb. 1999. The role of indicator species: neotropical migratory song birds. Pages 187–208 *in* J. D. Peine, editor. Ecosystem management for sustainability: Principles and practices illustrated by a regional biosphere reserve cooperative. Lewis Publishers. New York, NY.

Steel, Z. L., M. L. Bond, R. B. Siegel, and P. Pyle. 2012. Avifauna of Sierra Nevada Network Parks. Assessing distribution, abundance, stressors, and conservation opportunities for 145 bird species. Natural Resource Report NPS/SIEN/NRR—2012/xxxx. National Park Service, Fort Collins, Colorado.

Tingley, M. W., W. B. Monahan, S. R. Beissinger, and C. Moritz. 2009. Birds track their Grinnellian niche through a century of climate change. Proceedings of the National Academy of Sciences 106(suppl. 2):19637-19643.

NPS 963/116865, September 2012